EXPLORING CAREERS IN
TV AND FILM

Set Design in
TV and Film

Ruth Bjorklund

Cavendish
Square

New York

Published in 2019 by Cavendish Square Publishing, LLC
243 5th Avenue, Suite 136, New York, NY 10016

Library of Congress Cataloging-in-Publication Data

Names: Bjorklund, Ruth.
Title: Set design in TV and film / Ruth Bjorklund.
Description: New York : Cavendish Square, 2019. | Series: Exploring careers in TV and film | Includes glossary and index.
Identifiers: ISBN 9781502641526 (pbk.) | ISBN 9781502641533 (library bound) | ISBN 9781502641540 (ebook)
Subjects: LCSH: Motion pictures--Setting and scenery--Juvenile literature. | Television--Juvenile literature. | Motion pictures--Setting and scenery--Vocational guidance--Juvenile literature. | Television--Vocational guidance---Juvenile literature.
Classification: LCC PN1995.9.S4 B57 2019 | DDC 791.4302023--dc23

Editorial Director: David McNamara
Editor: Kristen Susienka
Copy Editor: Rebecca Rohan
Associate Art Director: Alan Sliwinski
Designer: Christina Shults
Production Coordinator: Karol Szymczuk
Photo Research: J8 Media

The photographs in this book are used by permission and through the courtesy of: Cover David Walter/Alamy Stock Photo; p. 4 ©Summit Entertainment/courtesy Everett Collection; p. 7 Goodluz/Shutterstock.com; p. 8 AleksandarGeorgiev/E+/Getty Images; p. 13 Tm Zml/Shutterstock.com; p. 16 Hero Images/Getty Images; p. 19 Thomas Barwick/Stone/Getty Images; p. 20 dpa picture alliance archive/Alamy Stock Photo; p. 24 David McNew/Getty Images; pp. 28, 40 AF archive/Alamy Stock Photo; p. 34 Dream Pictures/The Image Bank/Getty Images; p. 38 Michael Stewart/GC Images/Getty Images; p. 41 Georgejmclittle/Shutterstock.com; p. 43 Loraks/Shutterstock.com; p. 45 Raphye Alexius/Image Source/Getty Images; p. 46 Paul Briden/Alamy Stock Photo; p. 48 Valerie Macon/AFP/Getty Images; p. 52 Mondadori Portfolio/Getty Images; p. 56 Imtmphoto/Shutterstock.com; p. 58 LeoPatrizi/iStock Unreleased/Getty Images; p. 63 Chris Ryan/OJO Images/Getty Images; p. 65 BJones27/E+/Getty Images; p. 68 Simonkr/E+/Getty Images; p. 72 Sunset Boulevard/Corbis Historical/Getty Images; p. 78 Photographee.eu/Shutterstock.com; p. 80 Opas Chotiphantawanon/Shutterstock.com; p. 83 Sam Aronov/Shutterstock.com; p. 86 Kirk McKoy/Los Angeles Times/Getty Images.

Printed in the United States of America

CONTENTS

Before an actor walks on set, the set's design begins to tell the story.

CHAPTER ONE

Ready, Set!

Action! The film set is dark. A door swings open, and an actor enters. She flips a switch that lights up a room. What do you see? Is the room neat and orderly? Are clothes strewn everywhere? How about pizza boxes? Sports equipment? A piano? Children's toys? In that first instant, the film set begins telling you a story.

Who was responsible for introducing you to the story? The set designer—in large productions called a production designer—made it possible. It is the role of the set designer to ensure that every item on the set conveys meaning. Set designers make a television or film set come to life. To make this happen, they work with all members of the production team—actors, producers, directors, the camera crew, carpenters, sound and lighting engineers, and the set crew.

The Big Picture

Set designers must be both practical and imaginative. It is their job to immerse themselves in the storyline and support the actors. They must have the skills to create, communicate, and construct. Set designers understand the production's larger vision but perform their own role with detailed accuracy.

People pursue a career in set design from many avenues. Some people are interested in literature and drama, some enjoy carpentry or painting, while others are attracted to architecture or interior design. Whatever your strengths and interests, it is important to realize that you will need to learn a variety of skills to be successful in a set-design career. It may take some time to develop new skills and hone your natural talents, but a career in set design can open the door to an exciting new world.

Creativity

Set designers are artistic people. Whether their talent lies in painting a mural, building a staircase, or upholstering a chair, they express themselves in a visual way. They are drawn to acting, literature, and storytelling, and their contributions to the dramatic arts are wholly visual.

Set designers put their first thoughts on paper, sketching set layouts and a few set pieces. They may use pencil or computer-aided design (CAD) tools. There are several design software programs that might be used, such as Adobe Photoshop, AutoCAD, Adobe Illustrator, Vectorworks, 3ds Max, and SketchUp. Some of these programs have advanced features, and some are easy to use. Regardless of whether set designers draw by hand or use a computer, they must have a working knowledge of rendering, drafting, architectural blueprints,

Many set designers prefer to produce their layouts and blueprints by hand.

and basic construction techniques. A rendering is a drawing but not as precise as drafting, which includes measurements.

Set designers should know how the basic elements of design work. They must have the talent and skill to see relationships between color, line, light, shape, texture, and space. Set designers often begin with one of those elements and build outward from there.

Communication

Successful film and television productions are not possible without teamwork. All members of the production rely on the set designer to express

Set designers will check out fabrics in stock with the production team's upholsterer.

ideas clearly and concisely. The set designer's first responsibility is to read the script and develop a thorough understanding of the action, plot, mood, emotion, and most of all, setting.

Teamwork begins with a gathering of the production's creative team—the director, the costume designer, and the set designer. Early meetings establish the director's goals and visions. The creative team exchanges ideas. At the next meeting, the creative team presents their first ideas and impressions to the others for critique. For the set designer, this means being able to communicate verbally as well as visually with sketches, photographs, and layouts. Set designers also have ongoing discussions with carpenters, painters, sound and lighting engineers, the camera crew, and the set crew.

Construction

Set designers must have the ability to think three-dimensionally. Although their earliest presentations are flat drawings on paper, set designers produce blueprints showing layouts and elevations. After they are approved, set designers draw or use CAD software to make 3D drawings of the sides and top of the set. After many rounds of discussion and changes, the set designer will make a cardboard or softwood model of the set or sets. The model is expected to be a finished version, built to an exact scale of the actual set.

Besides having the skill to design blueprints, draft in 3D, and make models, a good set designer should know how to do basic carpentry, or at best, how well their construction plans will hold up to the rigors of use. Set designers also do more than provide or construct objects such as furniture, stairways, and streetlights. They must have the know-how to construct and define the borders of the set, such as walls, gardens, or building facades.

Other Skills

Not every set designer needs to be an architect, carpenter, or interior decorator. However, there are basic skills that people interested in the profession should be able to do, such as illustration, painting, and sewing. Most cardboard models, for example, are illustrated with relatively flat areas of the set, such as doorframes, shop signs, or artwork on the wall. There are numerous painting techniques that designers use to create depth to the set or highlight important scenes or players. Many objects have to be sewn and customized, such as curtains and upholstery.

Organization

Besides artistic talents, a successful set designer must know how to organize. They must know how to schedule shopping expeditions, carpenters' shop time, painters' availability, directors' meetings, and staff meetings (if there is a production design staff). They must be sure to factor in consultations with stage managers, lighting directors, audio and sound engineers, the camera crew, and the rigging crew. Most importantly, set designers must schedule adequate time for their own creative activities and production responsibilities.

Recordkeeping

When it comes to recordkeeping, set designers should think of themselves as "set production managers." Their responsibilities include a much wider range than designing a complementary and functional set. Set designers follow the production calendar and are aware of all the due dates. It is important that set designers meet their deadlines because if they do not, it affects the work of so many other people.

Set designers must keep very detailed records of their process, progress, and inventory. They keep files on all the items in their inventory. Most television and film companies have large warehouses called "prop houses" that store a wide variety of set elements. They have staging materials, such as walls, doors, stairways, and bookcases. They also keep a good stock of furniture, appliances, medical equipment, and electronics, as well as artificial veneers, such as fake stone or brick. Many set designers keep their own "go-tos," that is, a personal inventory of commonly used items such as dishes, pillows, lamps, rugs, tables, and chairs. The set designer will assess all the inventory and decide which items will be useful, which can be customized, and which will not be worth the trouble.

Shopping for set pieces is a major requirement of the job. Set designers must know where to purchase items large and small, old and new. They must keep records of which stores sell items they want and whether the items are in stock or can be ordered and shipped quickly. They also should note the best person to contact.

Once set pieces have been purchased, rented, or chosen, records must be kept detailing the work that goes into the final product, such as painting or upholstery. Set designers need to keep track of who can do the work—whether it will be a member of the production staff or an outside subcontractor, or if they will do it themselves. Each item should have a label indicating where it will be placed on the set and when it will be used. If you, as the set designer, are not available, other members of the company will rely on your notes to continue the work.

Budget

Television and film productions are expensive ventures, and everyone must be as efficient as possible. As a set designer, you do not want to be singled out as responsible for cost overruns! One of the most important qualifications a set designer must have is the ability to work within a budget. Beyond the most extravagant productions, most other projects operate on a tight budget. Money management includes the cost of purchasing or renting items for the set, upgrading and customizing objects, and paying for labor and materials. Many set designers work as freelancers. They need to have good accounting skills or hire a professional accountant.

Research

While set design is a very creative profession, it nonetheless has restrictions. Set designers need to do a lot of research before going to the drawing board. The first and most important part of researching is studying the script. Where will the action take place? A kitchen? A dark basement? A rooftop? A space station? Other important questions include in what time period does the story take place? What country, what culture? Is the genre fantasy, science fiction, or realism?

Once you have a foundation to work from, you refine your research. Set designers watch films and television shows and pore through books, magazines, and online sources like Pinterest or Houzz, looking for ideas. Some must travel. They visit museums, go to real estate open houses, and shop a variety of places—

modern and vintage furniture shops, hardware stores, craft and hobby shops, antique shops, yard sales, and secondhand stores.

Developing Your Skills

People can develop their skills and nurture their natural talents in many ways. It is a good idea to carry a sketchpad and spend time sketching every day. Be sure to take snapshots and/or write notes about interesting things you observe. Take art or shop classes if your school has them. Many community

Crafting and being resourceful are some of the perks of the job.

education or parks and recreation programs have drawing, painting, sewing, and/or carpentry classes. Crafting is another way to get involved in set design. There are many creative and useful craft ideas in books and online using paper, fabric, wood, beads, glass, inks, and other everyday materials. Some people may want to look for a summer job helping a building contractor or painter, or working in an arts and crafts store. You should keep a photographic record of all of your work. Include photos of drawings, models, sculptures, costumes, crafted items, and anything you have painted or built. You should also take photos of any of your work in school plays or videos and/or local theater. You may want to include some of the best in your résumé, either for a job interview or to enter college or vocational school.

Learn to Observe

Set designers should be aware of color, line, shape, light, texture, and space. If you keep those thoughts in mind and observe the world around you, you will begin recognizing how and why some things make a statement or make you feel something, while others do not. Notice how different colors call out for your attention while others seem to disappear. Colors also influence feelings. You may find yellow cheerful, brown depressing, and red exciting.

The design element of line may seem simple, but it is powerful. Think of vertical lines, such as a room with tall columns. Do you feel safe, intimidated, or uplifted? Notice how the horizontal line of a long table will keep your focus straight ahead. Zigzag lines, such as a crooked hallway or a garden maze, often suggest action or danger. Look around at various textures and shapes. What is more appealing, a soft velvet armchair or a weathered wooden rocker? What if the armchair is musty and torn and the rocker has a cushion?

Observe objects under different forms of light— sunshine, overhead lights in a supermarket, or the glow of a bedside lamp. And space, what might space tell you? Imagine interviewing for a summer job. In one interview, you are led into a large room with a desk and two chairs. But in another interview, you take a seat in an office crowded with bookcases and file folders. Does the large space make you nervous? Does the crowded space spark your curiosity? Developing the skill of close observation will give you a deeper understanding of the elements of design.

A set designer and a furniture maker discuss a design using a wood scale model.

CHAPTER TWO

Esprit de Corps

E sprit de corps is a French phrase describing the sense of pride and enthusiasm shared by people who work together. In any film or television production, such dedicated teamwork is vital. Nothing can move forward if ideas are not shared and work is not completed on time. Everyone must contribute their talents and skills to tell the story. The set designer is responsible for designing and overseeing how the set or sets are built. There is the artistic design work, the technical design work, shopping, painting, sewing, and construction. All of these activities require the cooperation and exchange of ideas with the rest of the production team.

From the Beginning

Set designers are essential to any production. They are part of the creative team, which is led by the director. After initial meetings, the set designer takes the director's vision and gathers ideas for the sets. During the next few meetings, the set designer presents those ideas for review. All other production departments, such as lighting, camera, and costume, need to know what the set designer has in mind before they can begin their work.

The director and set designer will discuss time period, style, and mood. Mood is the general atmosphere that the story creates, such as happiness, humor, sadness, tension, or fear. One of the biggest challenges for a set designer is to help with the mood of the story. For example, a colorful room with posters tacked to the wall could help create a funny mood. On the other hand, a stark white room with glass and metal furniture might suggest a tense atmosphere.

An important tool for set designers to express their thoughts is a mood board. A mood board is a visual collection of ideas that include color schemes, fabric choices, furniture design, set accessories, and architectural features. There are many resources set designers use to compile their mood boards. Some make physical mood boards by printing photographs, drawing sketches, and taking images from magazines. They mount these on presentation board and add fabric swatches, or sections, and samples of finishes such as wood, glass, stone, or metal. Some set designers make digital mood boards. They use software to design their mood boards and websites such as Houzz, Pinterest, and Matboard to gather ideas. You may already have your own mood boards on Pinterest. Houzz and Matboard are architectural and design-oriented websites.

As the set designer and the director come to an agreement about the sets, the set designer will produce blueprints and a three-dimensional scale model of each set. The blueprints and models are the basis

Set designers and others in similar industries convey numerous ideas with mood boards.

for future discussions with the other members of the production team.

Set and Costume Designers

The set designer and the costume designer work with the director to create a unified look and mood for the production. Set and costume designers use their sense of color, texture, and shape to highlight the actors and the action. Their frequent design meetings ensure that the costumes and the set complement one another. While colors and styles do not need to match or coordinate, in most cases sets and costumes

Costume and set designers work closely to complement each other's designs. This costume designer adjusts the costumes of actors filming a World War II movie.

should not be in conflict. For example, imagine a quiet, emotional scene in which the actors wear plain, neutral-colored clothing. The set designer's task would be to underscore the seriousness of the mood. But what if instead the set contained bold colors and clashing patterns? Wouldn't that be confusing and distracting to the audience?

Painters, Artisans, and Upholsterers

Most set designers, even in small productions, rely on the artistic talents of property makers, who are painters, upholsterers, and artisans who customize and decorate the set and set dressings. Set painters, known as scenic artists, have a variety of specialized techniques to create depth to a set. They may paint scenes outside of windows, flooring, furniture, and/or special prop pieces. They use special techniques, such as ones that make walls or furniture look faded and worn.

Furniture is used and reused countless times, and upholsterers are key to giving new life to used pieces of furniture. Many upholsterers work alongside sewers who stitch custom curtains, pillows, and other fabric pieces. Set designers call on artisans to create what cannot be found in stores or in inventory. The artisans work with plastic, metal, glass, and foam. As one set designer describes their work, "In the property-maker's room lives the wizard of the studio … an inventor, a chemist, a bit of an artist, and an engineer." In small productions, very often the set designer is that "wizard."

Set Dressings and Props

When you, as the set designer, have read over the script, you will sit down and take note of all the items the script specifically mentions. You will also note all the items you believe the set should contain. These items are called set dressing and include curtains, rugs, lamps, artwork, and personal items such as books, dishes, photographs, and knickknacks. The more detailed the set dressing is, the more realistic the set will be. Set designers also create sets that require specialized set dressings such as what you would find in a hospital, restaurant, mechanic's garage, or business office. On larger productions, set dressings are overseen by a set dresser or set decorator. Needless to say, set designers and set dressers work hand-in-hand. And again, on smaller productions, set designers also act as set decorators or dressers.

Hand properties, called "props," are the items an actor physically handles. A shovel, cellphone, hairbrush, coffee cup, or flashlight are examples of props. But a laptop resting unused on a desk or an umbrella leaning by a door, untouched, is a set dressing. Hand props are provided by a prop master. Prop masters read the script thoroughly and make notes of each item in each scene that an actor touches. The prop master's and set designer's responsibilities frequently overlap, so they work very closely together. On smaller productions, the set designer or decorator will handle the props.

Shop Talk

After initial rough drawings, set designers create more detailed plans. They draw blueprints that show the dimensions of the set and layouts. They also show the tops of things, such as the placement of each piece of furniture and structure—stairways, fireplaces, bookcases, appliances, or columns. The set designer also provides elevations, which are drawings that show the front and sides of the set pieces and walls. These drawings are shared with other production people—carpenters, artisans, painters, and stagehands.

Very frequently, set designers use custom furniture and set accessories in their sets. Carpenters, machinists, and artisans need to get accurate plans from the set designer as soon as possible, so they can get their work done on time. The first set of plans should describe how to build platforms, walls, and any large elements, such as pillars, stairs, and doorways. The next set of plans can be provided later. These will be drawings of smaller items such as a bookcase, cabinet, or bench.

When the set design is approved by the director, the set designer makes a scale model, called a white card model or a maquette. Building the scale model is a time-consuming process, and it must be accurate. It represents every 3D structure in the set, furniture as well as structures like columns, steps, changes in floor level, open doors, and railings. Flat set pieces such as curtains or paneling are sketched onto the model.

Like everyone else on set, rigging crews have to be resourceful when working on location. This man is setting up rigging for a cell-phone commercial.

Models are usually assembled using a scale of 1:48 or 1:50, meaning 1 inch on the model equals 48 inches or 1 centimeter equals 50 centimeters. The people who will be building the set or set accessories rely on the set designer's accuracy to do their construction.

Set designers also work with the rigging crews. Rigging crews build the scaffolding that holds up the sets as well as the platforms that are suspended above the sets. Riggers construct the systems of pulleys, wheels, wires, and ropes that move and lift set walls and pieces on and off the set. Riggers and set designers discuss the weight, shape, and size of the sets and the larger set pieces and how best to move them around.

PERKS OF THE TRADE: DIY!

Set designing offers many perks, and one is definitely the ability to access and nurture a sense of creativity. As a set designer, you will be asked to be creative every day, from small details to the big picture. You will be offered empty space and be expected to fill it with your vision. Successfully filling that empty space will give you pride in your achievements. Although you will collaborate with others in the production, you will be granted a great deal of independence to explore and create.

Set designers are devoted fans of DIY, or "do it yourself," projects. As British set designer Laura Payne declares, "It's just wonderful to look at something that you've made entirely from scratch!" Shopping in secondhand stores, painting backdrops and furniture, and gluing, stapling, nailing, and sewing random objects and scraps into convincing set dressings is a thrill for set designers. Robert Edmond Jones, legendary set designer and author of *The Dramatic Imagination*, described his career: "A set designer is a jack-of-all-trades. He [or she] can make blueprints and murals and patterns and light-plots … can understand architecture but is not an architect … can paint a portrait but is not a painter." Whether you are into architecture, interior design, painting, carpentry, or CAD drawing, you will use these skills and many more in every production.

The Techs

Colors can change wildly under different types of lighting. Set designers work closely with lighting engineers. There is so much to consider—not only the brightness or dimness of light, but the colors of light bulbs and filters. For example, you, as a set designer, want to design a set featuring a bright, orange, leather sofa. The production is a comedy, and your color choice helps set a light-hearted mood. But in some of the scenes, it is raining outside. The lighting engineer may want to use blue or gray light to suggest the weather. Your flashy orange sofa is going to look like mud under those lighting conditions. You and the lighting engineer will also discuss how the set design will allow enough room for lighting equipment and crews.

Likewise, you will work with sound engineers and electricians. Your choice of fabrics and surfaces, as well as how you configure the set and arrange the furniture, will have an effect on how sound carries. Soft furniture, draperies, pillows, and fabrics all help to absorb sound and reduce echo. Solid objects placed in the right locations can distribute sound more clearly. Set designers select light fixtures for the set, often drawing on their own inventory. Electricians want a light plan as soon as possible so they can wire the light fixtures or repair them if necessary.

Camera Crew

The set designer and the camera crew interact during the design stages and as the set pieces are being prepared and installed. The camera crew's concerns are space, accessibility, and mobility. There is usually more than one camera operator on a set, and the set designer needs to construct the set and arrange the furniture and set dressings so the camera operators can move about freely from all directions.

The Actors

The set designer should attend rehearsals and director's meetings as often as they can to get a greater feel for the actors' needs and movements. Rehearsals will give set designers more insight into the actors' characters, which will help to create more realistic sets. Actors frequently have ideas about what the set should include and often suggest changes or additions with the set designer and the director.

An art deco set and attention to detail were essential to designing *The Great Gatsby*.

CHAPTER THREE

Behind the Magic

Movies and television take us to worlds beyond ourselves. According to one designer, set design is the "secret behind the magic." The role of set design is to give depth to the characters, visually add to the plot, and bring the audience to another place and time. Sets establish time, place, and style and give clues to the tone and mood. According to one design instructor, "set designers create the space where actors roam."

Focus and Direction

Set designers partner with the lighting engineer to help the audience understand which actor or actors they should focus on. Viewers will direct their attention to the actor at center stage, rather than the person sitting in a corner.

Whether minimal or extravagant, a set design must help tell the story. Devorah Herbert is the set designer of the Netflix comedy *Grace and Frankie*. It is a TV show about two friends whose husbands leave them for each other. *Grace and Frankie* end up sharing a beach house and having many comedic moments together. Her producer says the beach house set is "the third main character." It visually shows how the two main characters manage to create a life together.

Set designers work within the limitations of space, time, and budget. However, it is often those challenges that spark the most original ideas and creations. Many set designers enjoy the opportunity to make something out of almost nothing. It sparks their creativity, and when their set or sets are completed, the feeling of accomplishment is very satisfying. Designer Courtney Cachet explains, "For some reason, the budget is almost never enough for what you need to do. Smaller amounts of money breed creativity you swore you never had."

Other responsibilities include interpreting and analyzing scripts, envisioning ideas, and then developing those ideas. Through various artistic means, the set designer presents those ideas in a clear and concise way to the director and the rest of the creative team. Following acceptance of the set design, the set designer begins choosing set locations, constructing sets, gathering materials, and buying, renting, or making set dressings.

Starting at the Top

Set designers begin by listening to their director explain what they want to accomplish through their ideas about mood, tone, and style. Some directors are very detailed about what they want, and others just want what looks natural or agrees with the story concept. Many directors emphasize one element, such as style, and ask the rest of the creative team to work from that point outward.

In the 2013 film *The Great Gatsby*, the director wanted to emphasize style—that is, art deco, the trendy style of the 1920s. The set designer, Beverley Dunn, researched the most famous European art-deco architects, interior designers, and artists. She used many antiques from the period, and when she could not find authentic furniture, she directed carpenters to build exact replicas. Her sets were compellingly lavish and true to her sources.

In the television show *Empire*, the main character is a wealthy African American businessman who lives an extravagant lifestyle. In designing his mansion, set designer Cece Destefano and set decorator Caroline Perzan used artwork created exclusively by African American artists and purchased a grand piano made by the United States' first African American piano manufacturer. Even though most viewers do not recognize such detail, Masako Matsuda, set designer of *Avengers: Infinity War* and *Jurassic World*, explains her thoroughness, "Of course the audience may not know about every detail … but if things are not done right, it won't look right. You may not know what it is, but you will feel it."

In the 2017 film *The Shape of Water*, director Guillermo del Toro wanted the set designer to focus on color to create mood. He and the designer, Paul Austerberry, looked at 3,500 color samples together. They chose just one hundred and assigned certain colors to each character in the film. The colors were used to define the characters' homes and workplaces. Color is key to developing character and expressing mood. Black or bold colors often define a powerful character, and neutral or muted colors often help define a modest, mild-mannered, or victimized character.

The set designer of *The Hunger Games*, Larry Dias, used tone to inspire his designs. A story's tone is how it makes a viewer feel. The tone of the film is tense and deeply unsettling. One of Dias's sets was a shared apartment that he described as "sort of like the Olympic village athletes' housing crossed with a prison." The set has lively, brilliant colors that are in stark contrast to the blunt, severe lines of the walls and furniture.

Read, Read, Read

Essential to designing a set is knowing the story inside and out. Many designers say they read the script the first time like a viewer would, for entertainment. They do not dive into details in the first few readings. Steve Saklad, who designs for film and television, says, "We only get a 125-page script that somehow has to express an entire world. We get to flesh out characters' backstories, design rooms with histories that go back generations, spot themes and story lines from Shakespeare to Marvel Comics. We have to interpret and connect these dots and use visuals to help an audience see these connections too."

Set designers "connect the dots" by dissecting the script and asking themselves questions, such as:

- What is the genre? (e.g., romance, mystery, comedy, etc.)

- How does it make you feel? (e.g., sad, excited, frightened, amused)

- Should we take events seriously or see the humor in them?

- What are some of the themes? (e.g., apocalypse, love, good vs. evil)

- What is the style of the production? (e.g., realism, romanticism, science fiction)

- What does the physical action call for? (e.g., an argument, a dance party, a robbery)

- Where is the action located? (e.g., New Orleans, outer space, Moscow)

- What time of day?

- What season?

- What sets are indoors? (e.g., living room, high-school hallway, police station)

- What sets are outdoors? (e.g., street scene, backyard patio, basketball court)

- What is the time period? (e.g., contemporary, eighteenth century, 1980s)

- Is there a specific era? (e.g., Middle Ages, Civil War, the future)

- How many characters will need to fit into each set?

- How many acts and scenes?

- How many sets will be needed?

A camera operator films from behind the "fourth wall." That is the area where film equipment and the audience are. Lighting and microphones hang from the open ceiling.

After answering these basic questions, set designers begin making lists. They carefully go over the script and write down any item specifically mentioned, such as an old bus, upturned easy chair, cash register, or fire escape. These items are called "hero props." Besides listing the hero props, designers list all the objects they feel belong in the set. Set designers make a list of all the major staging needs, such as walls and furniture. Another list will include all the items that will make the set convincing to viewers, such as a wall of family photographs, a cluttered bookcase, or a coffee maker.

Research

Set designers must research the elements of a script. Thorough research is especially important for sets that take place in another time period or in an unfamiliar setting. Libraries and bookstores offer a variety of books and magazines on architecture, interior design, and building construction. Designers pore over pictorial works on historical periods such as Elizabethan England, colonial America, the Ashanti empire, or ancient Egypt. Sci-fi graphic novels are excellent resources for futuristic sets. Set designers also watch a lot of film and television shows for ideas. If the setting is contemporary, many designers visit the location or read local newspapers and magazines. If the set designer is working on a major production, they may visit film archives in Los Angeles, Chicago, Washington, DC, or New York City. Set designers also gather useful information via personal interviews as well as from a tremendous number of online resources.

Location, Location

Many sets are built on a studio's soundstage or outside on a backlot; however, depending on the size or subject of the project, a set designer may be asked to scout out other locations, both interior and exterior. Sometimes, it is less costly to rent a building, especially a large or unique building, such as a restaurant, a snow lodge, or a luxury home on the beach. But finding the right location is not an easy task. There are many things to consider. The set designer and the director will make the decision together as it will affect the budget, the actors, and the production crews. In some productions, the set designer may choose to use both pre-existing locations and custom-built sets.

Budget, of course, determines much of what the set designer can do. Exterior location sets require permits. In some areas, such as New York City or San Francisco, the permit costs are very high. Time is another consideration. How much of a set designer's time is it worth spending on finding the right location?

When the set designer goes location scouting, he or she may spend many hours on the road or in the air, traveling. If you pursue the profession or want to try your hand at your own project, bring a good camera. Take shots of the sites from all angles. Bring good-quality lighting to get the best possible photos to take back to the director. If you have the time and the budget, try to find more than one option for each set. Accurately measure the sites—top to bottom, perimeter, width, and length. Check to see how reliable the utilities are, such as power, water, and internet strength. Take note of any physical features that may be problematic—a pillar, for instance, or broken windows. Pay close attention to sound. Does the space have an echo, or are there loud noises coming in from the street? Be sure to get a definite cost for rental and/ or permits before returning to the director with your findings and suggestions.

Some locations such as warehouses or abandoned buildings are popular, especially with low-budget productions. Such buildings generally rent for little cost, and sets can be built inside of them. Many set designers decide on locations that stand in for the "real" location of the story. The television show *Friends* was set in New York City, but the filming was done on set in Los Angeles. On the other hand, sometimes it is easier to shoot a film or television show in the "real" location where it is set, such as the television show *The Walking Dead*, which is filmed in Georgia.

Trying to find an unusual set location may cost much more than building a set from scratch in a studio. It can often be more cost effective for a set designer to build their own sets. When they build a set on location, they and the rest of the production crew are confined to the physical boundaries of the space. The set designer will have to design his or her set to accommodate the camera, rigging, and lighting crews. When they build a set from scratch, they can design it to make room for the production crew. The set will not have a ceiling so that lights can be hung from above. The set designer can build moveable walls so the rigging crew can make space for the camera crew to move around. Building a set gives the set designer freedom to design the placement of the walls, the floor

In the movie *Teenage Mutant Ninja Turtles*, actors wore special gear to film. They also worked with set designers to make the scenes come to life.

plan, the ceiling height, and any special architectural items, such as fireplaces or balconies.

Using Your Imagination

Nearly all of the set designer's work is done in preproduction. Set designers use their imaginations, but they often do so quite methodically. A set designer will likely spend several days sketching ideas and making notes. They will start organizing their thoughts and ideas into a mood board and a storyboard.

A mood board gathers a set designer's thoughts into what often resembles a collage. They communicate their ideas visually in the form of sketches, fabric swatches, photographs, torn pages from magazines, color palettes, samples of wall treatments (paint, wallpaper, paneling), flooring (wood, stone, brick, tile, linoleum), and other items that suggest the look and feel, or mood, of the set or sets.

You can apply these strategies of a set designer in your own life. Consider redesigning your bedroom or another room in your house. You do not have to spend money on new furniture, but you can take measurements and rearrange what you have. The fun of the project may also come from using DIY skills in decorating. You can look for inexpensive sources of materials to make bed covers, curtains, pillows, and rugs. Check out arts and crafts books and magazines from the library, and look online for ideas to decorate your walls, desks, tables, and bookcases. You may want to paint an accent wall or a mural. Find new ways to express yourself.

A set designer's storyboard is a more organized visual presentation of ideas. Think of a storyboard like a comic strip or a graphic novel. For each scene or act, the set designer will illustrate his or her thoughts about the set in which the action takes place. Sometimes it will be the same set in several cels of the storyboard, but the set designer will need to alter the set properties, such as a scene that is the aftermath of a party—chairs and tables in disarray, dirty dishes in the sink, used glasses around the room, a jacket thrown over a chair, or a pair of sunglasses forgotten on the coffee table. Set changes as seen in the storyboard will affect how the actors will move around the room in that scene.

You may want to practice making your own storyboard. Read a short story and map out how many scenes and sets you would need to build. Look for cues in the story that emphasize certain objects,

Directors and set designers use storyboards to visualize concepts. Here, director Alexander Witt reviews a storyboard for *Resident Evil: Apocalypse.*

light, mood, and/or color. Make a list of these elements and begin sketching individual sets in a series using your notes.

The Drawing Board

The earliest sketches were basically a set designer's thoughts in pictures. The next set of drawings will be a more specific visual account showing where the action will be centered, where lighting and cameras crews can work, and where to install major set pieces such as a sofa, an operating room table, or desks in a classroom. The next series of drawings, often called concept drawings, will include more detail—color palette, textures, and style, such as eclectic, modern, antique, or rustic. Many set designers still use pencil and ink or photo collages for these preliminary sketches, but more people are opting to use sketching software, such as SketchUp.

Once many of the concept sketches are refined, set designers begin drawing floorplans and layouts. Floorplans are drawn to scale and show a bird's-eye view of the layout of the set—all its lines, contours, and the placement of furniture and other major set properties. Although some people still prefer to draw layouts with pencil, rulers, and translucent paper, many now use illustration and architectural software, such as AutoCAD, Vectorworks, 3ds Max, Adobe Photoshop, and Adobe Illustrator. There are some versions of design software that are free to download. SketchUp is one of them. For practice, you could measure a room and its contents and experiment with ways to rearrange furniture and objects.

Along with the layout, the set designer provides elevations, which are scale drawings of set walls, structural features, and major set properties shown from the side. Combined, the layout and the elevations

A set designer uses different software programs to design 3D models of sets.

are called the blueprints. Most set designers today also provide 3D drawings of the set, and these are nearly always done using 3D-modeling software.

Models

Once the sketches and blueprints are completed, the set designer is usually expected to build a 3D model of the set, including walls, floors, steps, open doors, changes in floor level, and all major set properties. Directors, actors, and builders use the model as the basis for communication throughout the preproduction period. Models, called "white card" models or maquettes, are constructed using heavy white card stock, foam or tack board, or lightweight wood, such as balsa. They are built by hand using X-ACTO knives, scalpels, small jigsaws, and glue. For large productions with multiple sets, set designers may buy ready-made pieces, such as walls, furniture, figures, vehicles, trees, and streetlights, as well as other common objects. These are called scenery elements and help people get a correct feeling of proportion. Building a model is a painstaking process. Many people will be working from your model and rely on it to be accurate in scale and design. Design instructor David Neat said this about model-making: "If there is only one thing you remember from this information make it this—it will take twice as long as you think it will." All of this may change in the future. Many believe that white card/ maquette models may soon be made by 3D printers using CAD drawings.

A white card model is time consuming but an invaluable tool for helping others work with the set design.

Lining Up

The usual construction of a set is three walls with no ceiling. The missing fourth wall allows access for the director, camera operators, and lighting and rigging crews. Sometimes a set is just one freestanding wall if it is, for example, the facade of a building. Some sets built for scenes with light action, such as someone sitting at a desk or two people talking in a corner, might have only two walls.

Above all else, a set must support the actors and the action. You as a set designer will need to design your set accordingly. Proportion is very important. Will your set appear realistic with the characters in action? Remember, you are designing in three dimensions, but the viewers will see the film or television show in two dimensions. You should think of designing your set like you would compose a photograph.

One extremely important part of set designing is unfortunately not left to a set designer to decide. Where are the characters in each scene? How will they move across the set? In which direction will they move, and at what point might they keep still to deliver important lines? Deciding all this is called blocking, and it is the director's job. However, it is often difficult for the director to finalize the blocking when so many acting changes happen during rehearsals. You can only hope your set design will not require much alteration once the cameras start to roll.

Building Your Set

You should have the design and measurements of your major staging materials ready as soon as possible. Large productions will have a construction staff that includes carpenters, laborers, and painters, as well as upholsterers, artisans, and fabricators. Otherwise, set designers will hire and oversee independent contractors to build the sets. It is important to get your design plans to them quickly. In small productions, you will likely be in the mix—hammering nails, painting walls, refinishing furniture, sewing draperies, and crafting artwork out of metal and foam.

Shopping

Shopping for a set can be daunting. By the time most of the major design work is done, you, as the set designer, will have made a list of all the items you will need for your sets. One designer emphasizes "need" because no budget really will allow you to get all that you want. Of course, large budgets will allow you to shop for authentic antiques or high-end furniture. But often, designers have reproductions built. Set designers keep track of where to find certain types of items, from antiques, to knickknacks, to designer fabrics, to mid-twentieth-century appliances. Some designers keep a personal inventory of often-used items, such as rugs, lamps, chairs, or pottery. Many production studios also have a stock of set properties, called "prop shops," available.

However, it is expensive to store items. Sometimes, a set designer will purchase a major set piece that is featured in the story. Most other set properties are

Many set designers shop for set props in well-stocked vintage and antique stores.

rented, borrowed, or purchased used from Craigslist, estate auctions, yard sales, vintage stores, antique shops, and secondhand stores. Objects not found are constructed, or an alternative gets worked into the design.

Set Dressing

After the set structure has been built, the set is dressed. In many smaller productions, it is the set designer who fills this role, but in productions with larger budgets, set decorators or set dressers are hired to perform this job. Set dressing is the task of providing and installing furniture, decorations, and all the small details that go into making the set seem real. It is this part of the job where a set designer's skill in interior design comes to the fore.

The set dresser, or set designer, works closely with the prop master to be sure that all the hand

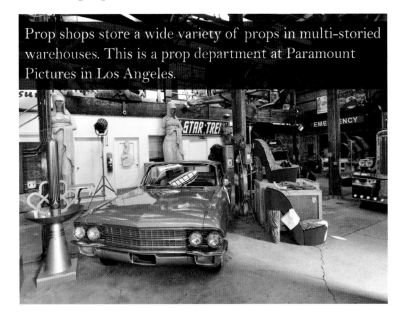

Prop shops store a wide variety of props in multi-storied warehouses. This is a prop department at Paramount Pictures in Los Angeles.

props and set properties coordinate. For example, there may be a scene where characters are in a kitchen drinking cups of tea (hand props), yet nowhere in sight is there a tea kettle (set property). Dennis Gassner, production designer of *Blade Runner 2049* and *The Golden Compass*, said, "You build environments for characters and define their space. That's really how we go about it."

The set dressing is very important to the actors. They not only need to move about freely but should feel comfortable in the set. Sometimes, small details help the actors stay in character. Set designer Rosemary Bradenberg says, "A lot of what we do is creating surround for the actors. I take that very seriously—making sure the actors feel like they can help build their characters out of what I provide."

During and After the Production

The set designer's role is often over once the filming begins. However, in larger productions, production designers and set decorators remain on hand for any of the director's changes. They also make sure that each new set or location is ready for the next shoot. Location and set prop rentals are expensive, so borrowed or rented items are returned quickly.

Before Beginning Your Career

There are many ways to get training if you want to be a set designer. The foremost way is to become a part of the drama department in your high school or community theater. Working backstage will give you

"I AM A DESIGNER, NOW"

Hannah Beachler wowed audiences with her set design in the Marvel film *Black Panther*.

A young Hannah Beachler fell in love with fashion design. She remembers dancing around her childhood home in Ohio wearing her grandmother's prom dresses. She loved sewing, but she also loved watching movies. Creativity ran in her family. Her father was an architect, and her mother was an interior designer. In college, she studied fashion design. She thought that was her future, but she later changed her major to filmmaking. She agreed to help a classmate in a small film. "We cleaned kitchen floors and painted things," she said, "But that was it. I did that design for this really tiny horrible show and I was like yeah, I want to do this forever."

After graduating, she moved to New Orleans, where a number of television and film companies were filming on location. She worked as an assistant set decorator and set dresser. But she really wanted to be a set designer. She convinced herself by saying, "I'm a designer, now." She believes that is the best way to promote yourself, saying, "in the film industry ... You kind of announce it to yourself."

Directors took notice, and before long she was the production/set designer for award-winning films such as *Fruitvale Station, Creed* (a Rocky sequel), *Moonlight,* which won the Academy Award in 2017, and Beyoncé's visual album *Lemonade,* which came out in 2016. In 2018, she designed the Marvel film *Black Panther.*

When asked about her work, she says, "I'm giddy with excitement. Because that's a production designer's dream, to really build these amazing places that don't even really exist."

practice in many fields—lighting, carpentry, painting, and stage rigging. Many schools have a student broadcast channel, and participating in set design will also give you valuable practice. People interested in sewing and crafting can often take classes through community education or from fabric and craft stores. There may also be painting and/or CAD drawing classes in your community. If you participate in a local theater production, you must coordinate it with your schoolwork. You will also need your family's support. Your friends will have to accept that you will not be able to socialize as much as you normally would.

You may want an after-school job or summer job. There are many part-time jobs that can tie into set design. Among them are retail jobs in arts-and-crafts stores, and fabric, furniture, and hardware stores. Small production companies film local commercials, and you may find work helping to dress sets. If you have successfully tried building models, you may want to contact architectural or construction firms to see if you could work as an assistant.

What to Study

There is no particular experience required to be a set designer; however, it is important to get an education and to hone your craft. Set designers have different backgrounds and specialties. Some have a background in architecture, construction, or interior design. Others have worked in advertising and graphic design. Set designer Ken Larsen says he knows one set designer who used to design airplanes. "There is no set rule," he adds. "The more education and experience, the better." He also recommends getting to know as many people in the business as possible. He says, "It's not who you know, it's who knows you." He advises people to put together samples, photos, résumés, websites, and business cards, "and politely stick them in front of anyone you can."

The skills involved in set design are so varied that what you begin studying is really up to you. Many people begin their formal education by becoming an art or architecture major. Some are English or literature majors. Persons interested in technology, such as CAD drawing or 3D printing, have many opportunities to study. Colleges and universities have several technology and computer programs, as do community colleges and vocational schools. You may want to apprentice yourself to a carpenter or building contractor. People who enjoy sewing and working with textiles may become an intern or choose a trade school or major in college in textile design. There are a fair number of colleges and universities that offer programs in theater arts, which include coursework in set design, rigging, and lighting. Additionally, there are colleges and universities that offer specific degrees in set or scenic design; however, many of them are graduate degrees.

But do not feel overwhelmed. Set designer Jen Chu says, "More important than the degree is having relevant skills and hands-on experience." Many set designers are successful without a degree in set design.

Set designers rely on others, such as the cinematographer and the director, shown here, to ensure their designs are appropriate for the film or television show.

CHAPTER FOUR

A Tricky Business

Set designers, as well as production designers and set decorators, can be "wildly under-appreciated," says HGTV set designer Emily Henderson. She laments that many viewers see sets as preexisting spaces, but that they rarely are. Instead, "every detail has been designed, coordinated, and obsessed over by a team of people that never get credit." It is true that set designers do not receive the accolades that directors, producers, and actors do, but everyone in film and television knows that sets are crucial to telling the story. The lesson here is that set designers must be passionate and dedicated to their work, and not in their profession for glory and fame. The design editor of the *Creative Bloq* arts journal, Julia Sagar, points out that "Sets seem invisible because an audience assumes that everything they see on a screen was already there. They don't think for a second that it was all built up from nothing. That's the magic of design for film: you're not supposed to be aware of it. It's all a trick."

Starting Out

Set designers love their work, but they admit there are many downsides to endure and rise above. Some of their challenges include budgeting time and dollars, exhaustion, frustration, income, and stress. It is a very competitive career, and getting a start is not easy. Future set designers need to be prepared to accept rejection, entry-level positions, long hours, and low pay.

Most newcomers, as well as more-seasoned designers, are not hired as employees, but instead are hired as independent freelancers. Many newcomers start out as an art/production department runner, or trainee. You can expect to be a runner or trainee for a while before becoming an assistant. A runner generally does not require many qualifications. The job entails running errands, distributing paperwork, answering phones, doing office work, arranging for meals and snacks, and making reservations for transportation and lodging. A trainee has more responsibility, but you must have qualifications to be hired, such as a background in visual arts, technology, or media, and you will likely need to provide a portfolio with your résumé. While being a trainee or runner may not be what you expected from a career in set design, these entry-level positions will put you into close contact with experienced professionals. It is up to you to make the best of it. Many successful people in the field got their start this way and worked their way up.

Perhaps your first job in set design will be as an assistant to a set designer. What does a set designer's assistant do? Generally, an assistant is hired to do a specific task, such as illustration, drafting, model building, or CAD drawing. Other duties can include keeping records of the set properties that are borrowed, rented, or taken from a studio's prop house; making arrangements with upholsterers, carpenters, and painters to see that work is done on time; and overseeing the return of any props once production is over. You will have learned basic skills as a trainee and a runner, and been given more responsibility as an assistant, but you will need to be patient while you are gaining experience and building up a good reputation.

The Newbie

The first day of any job makes people nervous, but the first day of working on a television or film set as a set designer may make you feel that you have landed in the midst of chaos. Likely you will know only one or two people, or maybe no one at all. As soon as you arrive, introduce yourself briefly to everyone. You may feel awkward, but first impressions are important. If you do not introduce yourself on the first day, you may find people too immersed in their jobs later on and not have the time to make connections.

No matter how prepared you are, you can count on making mistakes on your first day and for many days or weeks, or even longer, after. People say that the worst mistake you can make is to think that you should never fail. No number of books or classes can really prepare you for on-set experience. Every experience, every set design will be different. All you need to do is apologize for your mistake and ask how to improve your performance.

It is important to establish good working relationships early.

Time

The biggest mistake of all is to arrive to work late. Television and film productions are run on a tight schedule. Says filmmaker Evan Luzi, "From the moment everyone arrives for a cup of coffee to the second the last person drives away from the location, producers, assistant directors, and others are watching the clock and measuring how much time is left, how much time is to go, and what time it currently is."

While an ideal workday may be from 8:00 a.m. to 6:00 p.m., there are countless variations in the schedule. Those hours can speed by, and if you are not efficient, or if someone in another department has held things up, your eight-hour day can turn into an eighteen-hour day. Experienced set designers make a point of arriving early in the morning, by at least fifteen minutes. It is better to arrive early and have a cup of coffee while you are waiting for others than to have anyone forced to wait for you. Set designers can also expect to work late at night, early in the morning, on weekends, and on holidays. There are times when you, as a set designer, need to be at a meeting at 7:00 a.m. and you have a two-hour drive to get there. So, if you have trouble working long, irregular hours, you may lose your job. Kevin Allen, who owns a business managing set designers, says that set designers are dismissed if they show "an unwillingness to put in the time and meet deadlines in a very unforgiving business. Deadlines are critical in our business."

Set designers and the art production crews have to get their work done ahead of the rest of the departments. They have to research, design, and build mood boards and models. Film set designer Masako Masuda is bothered that "the recent trend is that [time to design] is getting shorter and shorter due to the studios trying to push and save money … and good design takes time."

Set designers working on television shows often work nine straight months. A twelve-hour day is standard. Episodes are shot one right after the other, and as one set is built, the last is struck, or torn down, and the next is being designed. Designers build standing sets, which are sets that remain for most of the episodes, as well as swing sets, which are sets built specifically for one or two episodes, such as a hospital room or a police station.

Expect the Unexpected

Deadlines are indeed critical, but changes can happen suddenly for numerous and unexpected reasons. Set designers must be flexible and meet their deadlines regardless. A director may decide to change the filming schedule, and then there is a scramble to get the set ready on time. "Sometimes the paint isn't even dry," says set decorator Crista Schneider, "and sometimes a director walks onto a set and says

Shooting on location requires a lot of extra planning. This crew is setting up to film on the streets of New York City.

everything is wrong and you scurry around like a crazy person to finish a new set."

Television set designer Jen Chu says, "You MUST have a thick skin to do this. The pace can be ten times faster than the pace of design in the real world, so sometimes orders are screwed up and mistakes are made, and you just have to stomp the fire out ASAP and keep moving. You have to be able to think on your feet and be willing to get your hands dirty." Film set designer Eve Stewart shared an example when she designed for the 2012 film *Les Misérables*. After all the sets were built and filming had begun, the director decided to film the actors singing live on the set, rather than dubbing the songs into the soundtrack. Suddenly, Stewart had to soundproof her entire set, which included houses, horses, and cobblestone streets. She had to find rubber props and cover the horses' hooves and carriage wheels with rubber. To further muffle the sound, she glued velvet to all the walls and laid carpet underneath the rooftops. All of this was done overnight!

Stress

Stress is a big part of the job, and set designers must learn how to handle it. Every day brings a new challenge, and a set designer needs to be able to do the job without getting rattled. Flexibility and self-confidence are necessary, especially when plans begin to unravel—bad weather delays a materials delivery; the set designer's choice of upholstery fabric is suddenly on back order; a rented set property gets damaged backstage; a director cuts some scenes and no longer needs the set a designer spent much time and money on. Kevin Allen says, "Set design, or any other creative profession, is not for the faint of heart or anyone with a fear of work." Arts journalist Ann Jackson writes in *New England Film* magazine, "If you don't like hard work, thinking on your feet, and large amounts of stress, being a set/production designer is probably not for you."

Budgets

Television and film productions operate on a strict budget. Set designers perform a huge juggling act, trying to conform to the budget. Besides taking into account the location of the sets, how many sets, how each set will be constructed, and by whom, set designers must determine how much to spend decorating the sets. Some TV show sets may be one or two simple rooms, while big-budget film sets can be extravagant, containing an entire village, an alien world, an Italian villa, or an amusement park. One of the most over-the-top set designs was built for the film *Waterworld*. The set was a 1,000-ton (907 metric ton) artificial island off the coast of Hawaii. It had countless problems, including being partially sunk in a hurricane. The cost overruns were enormous. Set designer Tom Lisowski warns, "If you are unable to deal with the money side of it, people are not going to want to work with you."

Raffy Tesoro, a set designer for TV commercials, says, "Every scale of film has similar problems and there never seems to be enough money to do what you initially plan. For some things, it always seems to come down to not enough time or money and often it takes a lot of thinking outside the box to manage and make it all happen."

Most set designers believe that working with smaller budgets is where you learn to be resourceful. Mistakes are easier and less costly to fix. Masako Masuda laughs, "Our joke is: we start with a mansion and end up with a shoe box house."

On smaller-budget television and film productions, a set designer can do it all—designing, sewing, building, sculpting, shopping, and set dressing. Beth Mickle, set designer for the film *Whiskey Tango Foxtrot*, explains, "On an independent film, everyone is moving and touching and painting everything … I'm always eager to grab the other side of a couch or to rehang picture frames on my own." Set designers working on big-budget productions almost always belong to a union, where there are strict dos and don'ts regarding what they can do. Set designers cannot pitch in and help paint furniture, hang paintings, or other such tasks. Besides protecting people's jobs, the union guidelines keep the jobsite safe.

Safety

Set designers are also responsible for the safety of people working to construct the set. They must budget for, and be aware of, safety codes. All flammable materials, such as curtains and fabrics, must be flame resistant. Chemicals are generally limited to paint, stain, paint removers, and glue. Trash should not be left around the set, nor any scrap lumber or other materials. Set designers should have a good understanding of rigging and the safety measures that go along with it. Set designers schedule carpenters, painters, and other set workers so that they can work at different times if possible and not get in each other's way while they work.

Pay

Set designing for television and film is a competitive career choice. Even positions as trainees and assistants are competitive. Until you have proven yourself, gained a reputation, and have experience, you can expect that you will earn an average income. Your income will improve once you have worked on enough productions. The highest-paid set designers are usually full-time employees of major film studios. Once you are eligible to join a union, you will have better income and benefits.

Most set designers are freelancers who generally earn less than company-employed set designers. They do not receive a regular paycheck and must move from job to job. They are also responsible for providing their own benefits. Masuda advises:

> *If you really want a steady job and steady paychecks, you are not going to be happy to be in this 'feast or famine' business. There are always ups and downs, and it is highly competitive. But if you have a strong desire to achieve what you want ... and you're willing to take certain risks, I will say go for it!*

Freelance set designers need to be able to market themselves and not become discouraged by potential disappointment.

Marketing Yourself

Freelance set designers usually must market themselves for each project. Helen Rasmussen, who designed the set of *The Last Samurai*, describes her experience, saying, "My first job was a 'word of mouth' recommendation. In my experience, the film business progresses in this way: you begin as an assistant in any department, hopefully one that interests you, and see how the process works. Then, you work hard and are reliable, and people remember. They remember even more if you are not reliable!"

Entry-level jobs are an important step in networking. Once you have worked with people and made a connection, you want to stay connected, person-to-person, and not just on social media such as LinkedIn. It is very important to learn the art of personal networking. Rasmussen advises, "Once you have been involved in a production, even as an assistant, stay in touch with the people you directly worked with. Find out if they know of upcoming projects and let them know you are interested in more work. Also, ask what else you can do to improve your knowledge." Kevin Allen agrees, saying, "We rely on simple, old-fashioned techniques like word of mouth and recommendations by colleagues."

As each new job presents itself, you must be prepared with an up-to-date résumé, solid references, and photographs and videos of sets you have worked on. After each job, you will have done something different and learned something new.

Bear those thoughts in mind when you update your résumé and prepare for your interview. When asked about being a freelance set designer, Paul Austerberry says:

> Really, there is little that I don't like, but certainly the amount of time spent actually creating is much less than the time spent managing and marketing the creativity. Everything has downsides … There are times when the continuous marketing can be a drag, but overall this is a great career.

While shooting a production, the set is always crowded with actors, directors, set props, and camera and lighting crews.

Getting Along

Erin Muldoon Stetson, a set designer in New York, has worked in a variety of productions with numerous coworkers. "Resourcefulness," she says, "is your number one trait, and being able to get along with people. Those two things can make anything happen." Getting along with people is a major part of success. Given that every production runs at a frantic and often stressful pace, it is easy for people to lose their calm and their manners. Jen Chu recounts, "With so much that has to get done in a short time frame, every now and then, personalities clash. I've realized that sometimes people hit a breaking point and you need to cut them some slack. I've learned not to take things personally and not to gossip about other people."

It is also important to respect people's positions and authority, even if they are friendly. One filmmaker writes, "Your boss may be your friend, but when the film is being made, your boss is your boss first … I've always been friendly with those I worked with, but when crunch time was happening, I treated them like they were my boss, and they treated me like I was their crew." In any production, there is a hierarchy, starting with the director, and you, as a set designer, or assistant set designer or decorator, must respect the "chain of command."

Everyone has a job to do, and a set designer who oversees the set-production process is essential at the start of the project and at the end. Everyone in every department is responsible for getting their work done on time. TV set designer Crista Schneider says, "A production is almost like surgery, [where] everyone has a specific job which must be done at just the right time." When there are delays, it is often the set designer and/or set decorator who is forced to meet earlier deadlines and must produce at the last minute.

Technology

Technology is rapidly becoming a necessary and very commonplace part of set design. For certain, some of the best and most experienced set designers "know their way around a pencil," but more and more technological skills are becoming a necessity.

Young people moving into the field often believe that having CAD drawing skills are what it takes to advance. Newcomers tend to rely on software to do their calculations and provide construction details to the production crew, carpenters, and other members of the stage crew. However, professionals in the business say that the newcomers need to be aware of and familiar with architecture and the "real world of set construction." Many computer-drawn designs are not necessarily going to stand up to use or look right on camera. Nor may the designs fall within budget restrictions.

There are two types of computer-generated imagery, special effects and CGI. Mostly, special effects are done on the set, such as fog or rain, and CGI effects are done after the filming is complete. Set designers today must work with the CGI people. Many designers see a benefit to CGI. For example, CGI can turn a one-story physical set into a 200-story building. However, digital technology and traditional live sets have many things to work out.

Another problem of traditional set design and the coming age of computer-driven set design is that the two techniques must be able to work together. Set designers do not all use the same software. There are no rules or standards. It can be complicated for set designers and art departments to swap files and exchange drawings, all using different software. Masuda says, "Our business is like being in a jungle."

Long Time Gone

Television set designers put in long hours during the course of a television show's season. Most seasons have twenty to twenty-four episodes. They are filmed back to back, so a designer is either reading, designing,

PENCIL VERSUS CGI

This television weather reporter is giving the weather forecast in front of a green screen.

An ongoing debate in set design is getting larger. Epics, fantasy, and science-fiction productions are increasingly popular, and set designers are grappling with the pros and cons of CGI technology. Experienced set designers prefer the realism of physical sets. Actors prefer physical sets, saying it is hard to interact with a "green screen." (A green— sometimes blue—screen is a solid color backdrop that CGI graphics are later added to.) Set designer Philip Messina says, "I love the look on an actor's face when they walk onto a set that I've created and they see the story that I'm trying to tell. You're telling a story with walls and paint and furniture. Green screen makes it more difficult to get into the role." He adds, "I feel like the CGI world can take over in a film very quickly."

Many fantastical and elaborate sets are difficult to design, but physical sets are no more expensive than digital sets. Messina describes designing an on-location Civil War-era set. Although houses on the street were historic, there were now telephone poles. Instead of removing them, Messina had them digitally erased. Three *Hunger Games* films were filmed at the same time in Berlin, Paris, and Atlanta. Messina had to rely on CGI to fill in the gaps. He pointed out that scenes called for a giant greenhouse, and all he physically built was the door. He says, "You don't ever want to shun CGI to make your life harder, but you don't want to use visual effects to be lazy about the craft."

prepping, or taking down sets. A twelve-hour day is an industry standard, even for union members. Often the day extends into fourteen hours, as there must be time allotted for cleaning up. A full season is frequently nine months long. That is a long time to be away from home. Even if set designers are working near where they live, fourteen hours plus travel time does not leave much time for family dinners, birthday parties, or lazy Sunday afternoons.

For film set designers, long working hours for weeks or months are also normal. Many films are shot on location, and cast and crew will be far from home and not able to see friends or family for most of that time. Annie Atkins, the set designer of the film *The Grand Budapest Hotel*, says, "Be prepared to live on the set!" Set designer Philip Messina points out that now fewer films are made in southern California, a traditional location for movies and TV shows. If you are working in film, he says, "It's very much like you're signing up for a life on the road … It makes it very difficult to have a career and a family."

Many people depend on the set designer to be available on the set. The director, prop master, set decorator, costume designer, and the construction crew frequently need to exchange ideas and make adjustments. Set designers attend as many rehearsals as they can to see how well sets function and how comfortable the actors feel in them. And of course, set designers need to be on hand when last-minute changes surface. A responsible and reliable set designer is going to have to accept being away from friends and family while working on a production.

It's a Wrap

People who work in television and film production spend a lot of time together and often get very close. You not only get to know people well working on a show or film for months, but television casts and crews can sometimes work together steadily for several years. "You go through a lot of stuff together," says Schneider. When a production ends, people feel tugged in two directions. You are excited for time off and to be with your friends and family. On the other hand, you will miss your TV and film family. But Messina puts it into balance, saying:

> Every time you start a new film, it's a fresh beginning. And with that beginning there's an end. There's an end where you all say goodbye to each other. Some people you're going to miss terribly, and some people you're happy to say goodbye to. There's a beginning and an end, and then you're off and you start another project.

The set establishes a mood on screen that helps tell the story. The actors of *Sleepy Hollow* worked on eerie and dark sets.

A Little Bit of Everything

Set designers need to know about architecture, construction, materials, project management, interior design, and literature. They must learn to draw, paint, and use technology. Says set designer Raffy Tesoro, "You need to know a little about everything. You're creating a world after all, down to the pots and pans, nails, bedbugs and whatever else is there no matter how big or small … you're a god … even if it's just for a little while."

Going Places

Set designers and their often-intermingled careers as production designers and set decorators have an enormous variety of talents and skills to take out into the world, if they so choose. There are numerous career paths open to them. Their skills in designing, conceptualizing, managing, budgeting, and building will open doors for them in many other professional fields.

Set designers who wish to find other employment are sought after in event planning, merchandising and display, architecture, construction, CAD drawing, and interior design. Many set designers may want to explore other television- and film-related careers, such as costume design, makeup, or directing. Alfred Hitchcock, legendary director of *Rear Window, Psycho,* and *The Birds*; Tim Burton, director and producer of *Alice in Wonderland, Beetlejuice,* and *Charlie and the Chocolate Factory*; and James Cameron, director of the epic films *Titanic* and *Avatar,* were all once set designers.

Architecture

Knowledge and interest in architecture has drawn many into television and film set design. The two careers have much in common. Many architects have found set design more exciting and attractive, while many set designers choose to abandon the stress of the television and film world to become architects. Both professionals take what is in their imagination and create a physical three-dimensional environment from a flat sheet of paper. The difference is that in architecture, the building is connected to the real world and must stand the test of time. In contrast, set design, along with set decoration and lighting, creates an illusion of reality for just a brief period of time. Philip Messina says:

> *I have a couple of good friends who are architects in Southern California—I joke that I have built more structures and*

more environments than they will ever have built in their lifetime, just because of the timeframe that they have to work with. And I get to design a greater variety of structures than they will have ever built—period houses, spaceships, post WW2 Germany, dystopian futures. I have friends that have spent 5 or 6 years trying to get a restaurant built!

Technical skills in 3D modeling and CAD drawing are essential skills for an architect, and many set designers have a good background in rendering technology. Additionally, an accomplished set design–model maker will be welcome working for an architectural firm. Many model makers are freelancers and contract to work for architectural and construction firms.

Graphic Design

Numerous types of businesses rely on good graphic design to increase sales and share information. Graphic designers are in demand for website design, advertising, publishing, and public relations. Take-away skills from set design into graphic design are numerous—beginning, of course, with creating something from nothing. Graphic designers, like set designers, start out with just a quick sketch or concept and by using line, color, shape, texture, and light, they produce a finished product.

Experience in set design is very helpful in building a career in graphic design. As a graphic designer, research skills help a designer understand his or her clients' product or needs, such as their target audience, market, and cultural elements. The client could be selling Yakisoba noodles, mountain bikes, or solar panels, and the graphic designer will know how to find ample background material on the subject. Like a set designer, a graphic designer will be able to communicate their design ideas clearly and have the creative and technical skills to give their clients what they need.

Many designers believe it is important to know and learn traditional techniques. They believe it helps develop a better understanding of art and how it is created. However, today graphic design heavily relies on computer-aided design. Most set designers—even those in large productions who have technology specialists on their staffs—have mastered at least one or two design software programs such as SketchUp, AutoCAD, Adobe Photoshop, and Adobe Illustrator. Computer-aided design makes changes easier and helps a set designer visualize ideas faster, with greater detail.

Technical Design

Set designers work with technology in their field, and some prefer to specialize in technology. Many set designers are experts in CAD design and drafting. They use CAD software to design their sets, make 3D models, and produce blueprints. There are a variety of fields for CAD designers and draftspeople, among them architecture, engineering, and construction.

Set designers do not produce CGI animation. However, they often work very closely with CGI technicians. Some set designers may be attracted to the field, but they must plan to seek advanced technical training to enter it. As set designers already know, CGI designers and technicians must be willing to work long hours, often under stress. If they are working on a film, they can be away from home for long periods of time. Additionally, CGI technicians, like set designers, are usually freelancers and may have to wait between jobs.

Construction

Some set designers may find a career in construction appealing. Besides actual building construction, other construction jobs include project management, marketing, CAD drafting, and design. A set designer has experience in budgeting, resourcing materials, scheduling, making and understanding blueprints, and many other skills valuable to the construction industry.

Interior Design

Interior designers and set designers share numerous skills and interests. They each use their creativity and research skills to design and oversee development of new environments. They apply their talents in design and technology, color coordination, furniture, fabric, and materials selection, as well as painting, construction, and decoration. Interior designers, like

Interior designers and set designers have much in common, but interior designers create an environment for real people, not characters.

set designers, enjoy working on a wide variety of interior spaces, including homes, restaurants, hotels, office buildings, hospitals, stores, health clubs, and libraries. Interior designers must draft and understand blueprints and communicate with clients, contractors, upholsterers, painters, and suppliers. They must know how to schedule work, control costs, and budget time. During the course of a project, interior designers must be flexible and able to solve unexpected problems, such as delays, cost overruns, and clients who make sudden changes. Accomplished set designers and interior designers share many of the same responsibilities and know how to take the good and the bad in stride.

Other Career Choices

Many set designers opt to earn a living in alternate careers by taking advantage of their wide range of skills. Television and film set designers are uniquely qualified to build sets for fashion and trade shows. Set designers know how to appeal to their audiences and create eye-catching backdrops for products. With skills in set design, a person can showcase his or her versatility and create fashion runways that range from the darkly dramatic to colorful and fantastical.

Set designers, with their ability to organize and create appealing environments, may find a satisfying career in retail merchandising. Designing displays for department stores, shopping malls, furniture showrooms, and boutiques can bring a former set designer satisfaction, not to mention regular hours and a regular paycheck.

Many corporate employers employ people with a set designer's skill to create stages and environments for conferences, events, and corporate retreats. Beyond designing stages and backdrops, many set designers oversee the entire event. Their skills in budgeting, purchasing, designing, managing workers, and meeting deadlines are very desirable. Many set designers choose to be event planners. Event planners design and manage promotions and special occasions, such as weddings, anniversaries, grand openings, and community celebrations. Event planners have to deal with many of the same challenges as set designers,

People with construction talents are well suited for designing and building gallery and museum displays.

such as long hours, stress, deadlines, strict budgets, and unexpected changes and delays. Many event planners are freelancers or own their own businesses.

Set designers who enjoy discovery and research may want to pursue a career in research. Many businesses and local governments rely on researchers to help them improve operations. Set designers with an interest in art may consider working for an art gallery or museum. Large museums have in-house exhibit designers, while smaller museums hire freelance designers. Museum designers and exhibit technicians require many of the same skills as set designers, such as knowledge of staging, carpentry, materials, and lighting, as well as budgeting, time management, and computer drafting and modeling skills.

You Have What It Takes

A career in set design blends natural talent with a wide variety of skills and abilities. The skills that you can develop while pursuing a career in set design can take you many places. Having abilities you can apply to a career in set design will also help prepare you for jobs in other fields. Take stock of your talents and appreciate your many advantages. Be aware of them and do not feel shy about educating any future employer about what you have to offer.

First of all, your interest and knowledge about literature, art, and history will help you be sensitive to people, society, and culture. Set designer Hannah Beachler says that the designers she has met are "travelers, explorers, and people who like to be challenged, people who like to understand other cultures and other people." When you are a reader, you are open and perceptive to others' needs and desires. These are important qualities in any field, whether in creating a museum exhibition of African art, planning a couple's dream wedding, or designing a family's new home.

The skills that people develop for a successful career in set design can appeal to other employers and suit other career paths. A good set designer knows how to meet deadlines. They know being tardy hinders a coworker's ability to get their work done and also shows a lack of respect. A set designer knows how to be available to others working on the set. Their ability to budget time and manage other's work schedules is necessary for meeting crucial deadlines. Any employer will appreciate an employee that is on time and completes work as scheduled.

While not expected in every job, a willingness to work long hours or be away from home when need be shows dedication to one's work. Maybe a person will not be expected to work overtime, but their job may require them to work hours other than an eight-hour day, five days a week. They may be expected to work weekends, evenings, and/or holidays. These hours are often a typical schedule for an event planner or a person who manages conferences or corporate retreats. Additionally, a person may find himself or herself working overtime if they must meet a client's deadline.

Set designers are masters at working under pressure. Stress can be a part of any project, especially in the final days before shooting begins. If a person develops the ability to remain calm and productive under pressure, they will become highly valued by any employer.

Many successful television or film productions expect the set designer/production designer to possess management skills and show leadership. Unless you are working alone on set design, you will have to learn to be a leader. A set designer in a large production may manage a design staff, as well as interact with other production departments. Many employers want to see leadership qualities in their employees.

A set designer knows how to negotiate buying materials for a set. Having previous set design experience could lead to a job in a purchasing

Fashion runway design requires enormous out-of-the-box creativity and imagination.

department of a company or as a buyer for clothing, furniture, art supplies, or hardware.

Knowing how to interact with vendors to get the best price and to have items delivered on time is a skill learned by set designers. The same skills will be essential to a job in a purchasing department. Set designers know how to keep good records of inventory and purchases and can follow up on shipments and deliveries. Many buyers travel to trade shows or fashion shows and frequently are away from home. Set designers and product buyers are accustomed to being out of town on location and are also willing to work irregular hours.

Person to Person

Working in film and television puts you shoulder-to-shoulder with your colleagues and other workers. If you are successful, you will know how to relate well to others. Teamwork is essential. Stuart Craig, the production designer for the nine *Harry Potter* films, said that a total of 588 sets were built by 86 artists and crew members. Without that teamwork, he said, it would have taken one person about seventy-four years to create.

Besides working as a team member, set designers also understand and respect the authority of the "chain of command" that puts the producer and director in ultimate decision-making roles. If you are considering a career in set design, it will be helpful to gain experience working on a school play or in community theater. If you do, you will start to develop necessary leadership skills. A position backstage on these productions will give you an idea of all the work that must be coordinated to get a production ready. You will likely take on many roles—upholsterer, sewer, painter, crafter, buyer, carpenter, and set decorator.

If you are working on a school play, community theater production, or local video shoot you may recognize you have the self-discipline to work independently. Every completed set will help you, as a set designer, gain more self-confidence. Your self-confidence and independent work habits may inspire you to own and operate your own business one day. With your knowledge in a wide range of subjects, you will have many career choices to consider.

Taking Stock

Set designer Erin Muldoon Stetson says her career is about taking the impossible and making it a reality. Consider how you can accomplish such a feat! As a set designer, you will have absorbed vast stores of knowledge that you may not even realize. The skills and abilities that you possess will appeal and impress any employer. Take stock of your strengths: awareness, communication skills, dedication, financial budgeting skills, flexibility, independence, purchasing skills, recordkeeping, resilience, teamwork, time, management skills, and the ability to work under pressure.

Set design is sometimes a labor of love. The work can be stressful, the hours long, and the competition fierce. On the other hand, a well-done set, whether on an award-winning film, a popular television show, or a small, independent production, makes it all very worthwhile. Set design calls for so many strengths and interests—literature, conceptualizing, drawing, modeling, construction, assembling, and decorating. Successful set designers do not need to be naturally talented in all of these categories, but they must train themselves to master many skills. They also must master basic business skills such as technology, budgeting, recordkeeping, communication skills, and personnel management. But as set designer Kevin Lee advises, "If your career is the pursuit of a passion, you will always be happy. That mental state of mind is priceless, and while there are no guarantees, it is highly possible that you will achieve success."

PACKING A PUNCH

Designer Kyle Schuneman is young but has an immense wealth of knowledge about the design industry.

Kyle Schuneman was born and raised in Chicago. Although the family's home was small, Schuneman's mother decorated it with style. His first job in set design was as an assistant for a Super Bowl commercial. However, he was determined, and in 2006, at the age of twenty-one, he scored his first design job for a set on HGTV. It was not easy, and being young did not help. He said, "There were tons of meetings, drawings, and whatever I could do to fight for the job, which I finally got."

After working as a set designer for a few years, Schuneman decided to expand into interior design. He quickly became a trendsetter. He was hired by major corporations to design events and displays. Although wealthy clients sought him out, he felt that he wanted to create interiors for small spaces, such as Los Angeles cottages or tiny New York City apartments. Schuneman attributes his experience in set design when he talks about doing interiors: "You have to pack a punch in a small space. It's my job to tell a rich story about the 'character' who lives in the space." He writes a DIY column and has designed his own furniture line. In 2012, he published a top-selling book called *The First Apartment Book: Cool Design for Small Spaces.*

Schuneman is a writer, interior designer, decorator, DIY crafter, and sometimes, still a set designer. When asked about his favorite occupation, he answers that it is set design because "you get to create a story and I love that."

GLOSSARY

backlot A large, undeveloped area on studio property used for constructing open-air sets.

blueprints Technical drawings that show the layout and elevations with measurements to scale.

CAD An acronym meaning computer-aided design. The software creates two- and three-dimensional plans and drawings.

cel A panel in a storyboard.

CGI An acronym for computer-generated imagery, which is software that uses digital 3D graphics to enhance special effects.

creative team The group of artistic collaborators, such as the director and costume and set designers.

director The principal creative artist on a movie or television set.

elevation A drawing to scale that shows the front or side of something.

go-to Any set prop that you store and keep in inventory.

hero prop A prop that gets a lot of screen time and is almost a character. A hero prop is always described in the script.

layout A drawing that shows a floor plan from above.

location The site of a set that is not built on a soundstage or backlot.

mood board A collage that communicates the look and feel of the television show or film.

overrun An instance where a budget or money has gone over the anticipated amount.

prop An object used in a production that is physically handled by actors.

prop house A large studio warehouse that stores set properties and hand props.

prop master A person responsible for purchasing, renting, manufacturing, and arranging on the set all props handled by actors.

rendering A perspective drawing of a design.

rigging crew Workers responsible for setting up set walls, lighting, and scaffolding on film sets.

set dresser The person who gathers the objects to go onto a set and arranges them in the proper location; also known as a set decorator.

set property A moveable object used to decorate a set; also called a set prop.

soundstage A large undeveloped area in a studio's building used for constructing interior sets.

special effect A mechanical or physical effect used on a set, such as rain, fog, or fire.

standing set A set that is used repeatedly in a production, especially in a television series.

storyboard A sequence of drawings that describe each scene in a film production.

swing set A set that is used only once or twice.

veneer Material stuck to a film set to give the illusion of an outdoor building material such as wood or brick.

white card model A 3D model of a set made from white cardboard or lightweight wood; also called a maquette.

FOR MORE INFORMATION

Books

Ackland-Snow, Terry, and Wendy Laybourne. *The Art of Illusion: Production Design for Film and Television.* Marlborough, UK: Crowood Press, 2018.

Adler, Phoebe. *Behind the Scenes: Contemporary Set Design.* London, UK: Black Dog Publishing, 2012.

Bailey, Diane. *Scenery and Set Design.* High School Musicals. New York: Rosen Central, 2010.

Barnwell, Jane. *Production Design for Screen: Visual Storytelling in Film and Television.* New York: Bloomsbury Visual Arts, 2017.

Culver, Sherri Hope. *Media Career Guide: Preparing for Jobs in the 21st Century.* New York: Bedford/St. Martin's Press, 2017.

Architectural Digest – Set Design
http://architecturaldigest.com/celebrity-style/set-design

Architectural Digest magazine regularly features articles on set design, which are available online.

Art Directors Guild
http://adg.org

The Art Director's Guild is a major international art directors' union. This website features links to resources, job listings, and reference materials.

School Video News
http://svnfilm.com

School Video News is an e-magazine for K-12 video production, including technical articles and descriptions of school projects and productions.

Videos

Black Panther Set Breakdown
https://youtu.be/EqKX1o9GkjM

In this television interview by 504 TV show, *Black Panther* production designer Hannah Beachler walks a viewer through M'Baku's throne room.

The Shape of Water Featurette—Set Design: The Chamber
https://youtu.be/sRjp-qLQo1c

Here you will find video clips and behind-the-scenes information about set designing the Academy Award–winning film *The Shape of Water.*

Online Articles

Azzarito, Amy. "We Want Your Job: Set Designer." Design Sponge. Accessed April 10, 2017. http://designsponge.com/2014/03/we-want-your-job-set-designer.html.

Bruney, Gabrielle. "Meet the Woman Behind Africa's Utopia in Black Panther." *Vice.* February 16, 2018. https://www.vice.com/en_us/article/3k7aj9/meet-the-woman-behind-the-african-utopia-in-black-panther.

Grouchnikov, Kirill. "The Art and Craft of Set Design: Interview with Masako Masuda." Pushing Pixels. July 20, 2013. http://pushing-pixels.org/2013/07/20/the-art-and-craft-of-set-design-interview-with-masako-masuda.html.

Neat, David. "1:10 Scale Furniture Models." davidneat.wordpress.com. October 18, 2017. https://davidneat.wordpress.com/2017/10/18/110-scale-furniture-models.

Watercutter, Angela. "How the Hunger Games Designer Built Its Epic Dystopian World." *Wired.* November 19, 2015. https://www.wired.com/2015/11/designing-the-hunger-games.

INDEX

Page numbers in **boldface** are illustrations

ABOUT THE AUTHOR

Ruth Bjorklund lives on Bainbridge Island, Washington. The author of numerous books, she has a master's degree in library and information science from the University of Washington. A versatile author, she has written books on subjects as diverse as state history, theater, world cultures, and the internment of Japanese Americans during World War II.